The Fort Lee Business Owner's Guide to IT Support Services and Fees

COMPUTER SYSTEMS ANALYSIS & DESIGN

The Fort Lee Business Owner's Guide to IT Support Services and Fees

What You Should Expect to Pay for IT Support for Your Business

(And How to Get Exactly What You Need Without Unnecessary Extras, Hidden Fees, and Bloated Contracts)

Larry Kahm, President
Heliotropic Systems, Inc.

Heliotropic Systems, Inc.
2000 Linwood Ave – Suite 19J
Fort Lee, NJ 07024
www.heliotropicsystems.com

Printed in the United States of America

ISBN 978-1-387-71684-5

First Edition

Dedication

My thanks to Robin Robins, of Technology Marketing Toolkit, for insisting that an IT services provider who has published a book stands as a thought leader in the community, and is "head and shoulders" above those who do not.

Table of Contents

Preface

Never Ask An IT Services Company, "What Do You Charge For Your Services?" Instead You Should Ask, "What Will I *Get* For My *Money*?"

From the desk of: Larry Kahm, President
Heliotropic Systems, Inc.

Dear Fellow Business Owner,

My name is Larry Kahm, President of Heliotropic Systems and author of an IT blog and numerous reports and books similar to this one to help business owners "snack" on condensed bits of IT advice. I have been providing outstanding IT services to businesses in the Fort Lee area for 10 years now. You may not have heard of me before, but I'm sure you're familiar with one or more of the other local businesses who are clients of mine.

One of the most common questions I get from new prospective clients calling my office is "What do you guys charge for your services?" Because this is such a common question — and a very important one to address — I decided to write this book for three reasons:

First, I wanted an easy way to answer this question and to educate all prospective clients who come to me on the most common ways IT services companies package and price their services, and the pros and cons of each approach.

Second, I wanted to bring to light a few "industry secrets" about IT service contracts and service level agreements (SLAs) that almost no business owner thinks about, understands, or knows to ask about when evaluating IT service providers. Sometimes these can end up burning you with hidden fees and locking you into a long-term contract when they are unwilling or unable to deliver the quality of service you need.

Third, I wanted to educate business owners on how to pick the *right* IT services company for their specific situation, budget, and needs based on the *VALUE* the company can deliver, not just the price, high OR low.

In the end, my purpose is to help you make the <u>most informed decision possible</u> so you end up working with someone who helps you solve your problems and accomplish what you want in a time frame, manner, and budget that is right for your business.

Dedicated to serving you,

Larry Kahm

Chapter 1: The "One Word" is Not Plastics, It's Computers

Because you are reading a book about IT support and services, you might think I was a computer "geek" from way back. Sorry, you're not even close.

I graduated from college with a degree in English; only I didn't start out on that path. I was planning to go into the medical field having enjoyed the details involved with genetics. But in my sophomore year, when I had to take Organic Chemistry, Physics, and Molecular Biology – all with labs and an incredible workload – I crumpled. There simply weren't enough hours in the day to read the books, conduct the tests, write up the results, and comprehend all of that information. Within a month I had become a wreck, unable to get better than C's and D's where I had previously been a solid B+ student.

I spoke with one of the career counselors in the middle of the semester and said, "Look, I can't do this. What else can I take that will let me graduate in the time I have left?" We reviewed various course offerings and the only option was English, with a minor in Education.

I found it significantly easier to take five courses at time and read more than 100 books in a semester than to take three courses with their associated labs. Nevertheless, I wrote papers that analyzed novels, plays, poetry, and short stories using the same techniques I had employed in the science classes I had abandoned. That approach caused some consternation with my instructors, but I insisted.

After college I discovered what it was like to find a job "in the real world" with a degree in English. I cursed that career counselor, because tough didn't begin to describe it. I eventually landed a job at a subsidiary of the publisher Harcourt Brace that conducted educational testing.

The organization used very old IBM equipment – punch cards and wired boards – items you would find in computer museums. About one year after I started work, the company had to get a new scanner to put the completed test results on tape, because IBM could no longer obtain replacement parts for the existing scanner to punch cards.

When the lead project manager ran into difficulties getting the new equipment to work I volunteered to help. I read the manual and tried the test sheet. It didn't work. Repeated tests also failed. It seemed strange to me that something that should have been so simple would present such a problem. So I tossed aside the manual and tried a different approach – and it worked.

When management asked what I had done, I explained that the manual had two steps in the wrong order and was missing one. I was only able to arrive at my successful result by testing several possibilities and discovering a pattern of what worked and what didn't.

After that episode I petitioned to take evening computer courses at NYU's School of Continuing Education. It took some convincing, but management eventually agreed. I actually enjoyed learning how to analyze problems – basically how to "think like a computer" – and to write programs. I enjoyed the challenges and solving those puzzles. With my literary background I quickly grasped the concept that writing a program is nothing more than listening to the requirements, understanding the business need, and then devising a solution – a series of instructions – that a computer could follow.

Over the ensuing decade I kept sharpening those skills as I moved from job to job. I went from being a technical writer, documenting data center operational procedures, to being a program administrator of one of IBM's more unusual problem and change management offerings. From there I became a project manager, evaluating software program products for use by application programmers. Afterwards, I became an expert on change management software and systems used by different entities within large corporations. I even became the local "go to guy" for application development on what was then a still relatively new device, the IBM PC running OS/2.

I slowly and resolutely increased the scope of my responsibilities and learned more about how computer systems were used in Fortune 100 companies. Of course many of them are now defunct or subsumed in some other company, but they included Manufacturers Hanover Trust, EF Hutton, Insurance Services Office, Merrill Lynch, Morgan Guarantee Trust, and Smith Barney.

During that journey my goals were simple. I had the desire to help people with the knowledge I was always discovering, and I was driven to provide them with the appropriate tools to help them solve the puzzles that computers presented.

Over the years I worked with application programmers, systems programmers, and management. All of this came to a miraculous juncture during the years leading up to the Year 2000 event. I was called by IBM to join their team of consultants at the New Jersey office of Paine Webber to assist with their Y2K conversion efforts. I wrote custom code, developed and documented dozens of procedures, and conducted presentations for hundreds of staff. It was the high point of a long career that had started quite inadvertently.

Afterwards, I continued to work on several similar Wall Street-related projects as Paine Webber transitioned into UBS.

A few years later I used those same skills at AIG for some of their expansion projects. It was during those projects that I witnessed first-hand the effects of "offshoring" office workers. As a result of being downsized, colleagues were no longer working and most were clamoring to find new jobs. Because I was the one person who knew about personal, mid-range, and mainframe computers, those former colleagues would often call me for help when they were suddenly working on their own, or from home, without the normal support of help desk technicians.

By the economic meltdown of 2008, I had had enough of the corporate environment. I needed to work for – and by – myself. The best approach I could envision was to provide computer services and support for small business owners and entrepreneurs. I recognized that they were working furiously to keep their businesses running, and they didn't want to be bothered with problems that invariably came up when using computers. So, using the key skills I learned a long time ago, and honed over nearly two decades in the Fortune 100 world, I revised an old and proven technique for a new clientele.

Now I meet with small business owners and listen as they describe their business. Using the simplest questions like "How?" and "Why?" I drill down to discover the problems they have and the goals they would like to achieve. Based on my interview, I conduct a thorough technology assessment of their business. Following that, I can devise the necessary computer solutions to help them. In essence, this is just like my early days of learning computer programming. I thrive knowing that I when I see the puzzle, I can study it and analyze its components, and then arrive at a solution that will benefit my clients.

With that as background, let's discuss what that entails.

Chapter 2: A Brief History of Computer Support for Businesses...

For you to understand what "Managed Services" is, and why it's so commonly used today, I want to take you back in time just a little bit.

Not too long ago, computers were very large and cumbersome, and used only by large organizations like corporations, universities, and banks. But by the end of the 1980s, many schools had purchased their first computers, and word processors were becoming common in offices everywhere. And by the mid-1990s, computers had become an indispensable part of everyday life. Of course, as the use of computer technology increased by all sorts of businesses, the need for computer support also rose.

For all intents and purposes, computer support basically started with "break-fix."

If something broke, the client called and (hopefully) the IT company went running to fix it. This was the way I operated Heliotropic Systems in the beginning, too. I used to go help anyone and everyone — basically waiting for the phone to ring. You must be thinking like I was after a while... There's got to be a more responsive, predictable way to solve computer problems so that IT support companies are not constantly waiting for help.

So IT companies developed procedures to go on-site to repeat clients, doing system reviews to look for *hints of problems* before they became too big. But the main problem with that — as you can guess — was that technicians could only see what was happening on that particular day.

The practice of Managed Services for computer support came soon afterwards as vendors developed software that would monitor computer systems just like technicians did. After all, the concept of outsourcing specific tasks to a specialist in one field had been around in other areas. In fact, you've probably had some form of managed services for your business for quite some time. PSE&G for your heat and electric is one. Spectrum or Verizon for your phone and/or internet are two others.

Businesses like yours realized that their network needs could be *effectively* outsourced to specialists in the IT field. New tools were being developed so that the day-to-day management of a business' computer network could be done by specialists outside of the walls of the business. This *strategic* "managed services for business IT" method would improve a business' operation by providing a higher quality of support, faster response times to users when needed, and yes, even cut expenses.

Chapter 3: Comparing Apples to Apples – The Predominant IT Service Models Explained

Before you can accurately compare the fees, services, and deliverables of one IT services company to another, you need to understand the three predominant service models most of these companies fit within. Some companies offer a blend of all three, while others are strict about offering only one service plan. **The three predominant service models are:**

Time and Materials

In the industry, we call this "break-fix" services. Essentially you pay an agreed-upon hourly rate for a technician to "fix" your problem when something "breaks." Under this model, you might be able to negotiate a discount based on buying a block of hours. The scope of work may be simply to resolve a specific problem (like removing malware), or it may encompass a large project, like a computer network upgrade or move, that has a specific result and end date clarified.

Note: Some companies will offer staff augmentation and placement under this model as well.

Managed IT Services

This is a model where the IT services company takes the role of your "IT department" and not only installs and supports all the devices and computers that connect to your server(s), but also offers phone and on-site support, antivirus, security, backup, and a host of other services to monitor and maintain the health, speed, performance, and security of your computer network.

Software Vendor-Supplied IT Services

Many software companies will offer IT support for their customers in the form of a help desk or remote support for an additional fee. However, these are typically scaled-back services, limited to troubleshooting their specific application and NOT your entire computer network and all the applications and devices connected to it.

If your problem resides outside of their specific software or the server it's hosted on, they can't help you and will often refer you to "your IT department." While it's often a good idea to buy some basic-level support package with a critical software application you use to run your business, this is not enough to provide the full IT services and support most businesses need to stay up and running.

When looking to outsource your IT support, the two service models you are most likely to end up having to choose between are the "managed IT services" and "break-fix" models. Therefore, let's dive into the pros and cons of these two options, and then the typical fee structure for both.

Chapter 4: Managed IT Services vs. Break-Fix: Which is the Better, More Cost-Effective, Option?

You've probably heard the famous Benjamin Franklin quote, "An ounce of prevention is worth a pound of cure."

I couldn't agree more — and that's why it's my sincere belief that the managed IT services approach is, by far, the most cost-effective, smartest option for any small business.

The only time I would recommend a "time and materials" approach is when you already have a *competent* IT person, or team, *proactively* managing your computer network and simply have a specific IT project to complete that your current in-house IT team doesn't have the time or expertise to implement (e.g., a network upgrade or installing a backup solution).

Outside of that specific scenario, I do not think the break-fix approach is a good idea for general IT support for one very important, fundamental reason: **you'll ultimately end up paying for a pound of "cure" for problems that could have easily been avoided with an "ounce" of prevention.**

Chapter 5: Why Regular Monitoring and Maintenance is Critical for Today's Computer Networks

The fact of the matter is computer networks absolutely, positively, need ongoing maintenance and monitoring to stay secure. The ever-increasing dependency we have on IT systems and the data they hold — not to mention the *type* of data we're now saving digitally — have given rise to very smart and sophisticated cybercrime organizations who work around the clock to do one thing: *compromise your networks for their illegal activities.*

In most cases their intent is to access financial information and passwords to rob you (or your clients), create fake identities for credit card fraud, etc. In other cases they may want to use your computer network to send illegal spam, host pirated software, spread malware, and so on. Some do it just for the "fun" of being able to make computer systems inoperable. These criminals work around the clock in teams, constantly finding and inventing new ways to get around your antivirus software and firewalls; that's why you have to remain ever vigilant against their attacks.

Of course, this doesn't even take into consideration other common disasters, such as rogue employees, lost devices, hardware failures (which are the number one reason for data loss), fire and natural disasters, and a host of other issues that can interrupt or outright destroy your IT infrastructure and the data it holds. Then there's regulatory compliance for any business hosting or touching credit card or financial information, medical records, and even client contact information such as e-mail addresses.

Preventing these problems and keeping your systems up and running (which is what managed IT services is all about) is a **LOT less expensive to your organization** than waiting until one of these things happens and then paying for emergency IT services to restore your systems to working order (break-fix).

Chapter 6: Should You Just Hire a Full-Time IT Manager?

In most cases, it is simply not cost-effective for companies with fewer than 40 employees to hire a full-time IT person, because you can outsource this function of your business for far less money and with a lot less work. But you DO want to hire an IT professional to perform basic maintenance just as you would hire an attorney to handle your legal matters, or an accountant to prepare your taxes.

If you truly understand the cost of your TIME and factor in employee productivity, the managed IT services model is considerably less expensive over time than the break-fix model.

Chapter 7: Why Break-Fix Works Entirely in the Consultant's Favor, *Not* Yours

Under a break-fix model, there is a fundamental conflict of interest between you and your IT firm. The IT services company has no incentive to stabilize your computer network or to resolve problems quickly because they are getting paid by the hour; therefore, the risk of unforeseen circumstances, scope creep, learning curve inefficiencies, and outright incompetence are all shifted to YOU, the customer. Essentially, the more problems you have, the more they profit, which is precisely what you DON'T want.

Under this model, the IT consultant can take the liberty of assigning a junior (lower-paid) technician to work on your problem who may take two to three times as long to resolve an issue that a more senior (and more expensive) technician may have resolved in a fraction of the time. There is no incentive to properly manage the time of that technician or their efficiency, and there is every reason for them to prolong the project and to find MORE problems than solutions. Of course, if they're ethical and want to keep you as a client, they *should* be doing everything possible to resolve your problems quickly and efficiently; however, that's akin to putting a German shepherd dog in charge of watching over a plate of roast beef sandwiches. Not a good idea.

Second, it creates a management problem for you, the customer, who now has to keep track of the hours they've worked to make sure you aren't getting overbilled. Because you often have no way of really knowing if they've worked the hours they say they have, it creates a situation where you really, truly, need to be able to trust they are being 100% ethical and honest, AND tracking THEIR hours properly (not all do).

And finally, it makes **budgeting for IT projects and expenses a nightmare** because your costs may be zero one month and thousands the next.

Chapter 8: What to Look For in a Managed IT Services Agreement and What You Should Expect to Pay

Important! Please note that the following price quotes are industry averages based on a recent IT industry survey conducted of over 900 different IT services firms. I am providing this information to give you a general idea of what most IT services firms charge, and to help you understand the VAST DIFFERENCES in service contracts that you must be aware of before signing on the dotted line.

Please understand that this does NOT reflect my pricing model or approach, which is simply to understand exactly what you want to accomplish FIRST, and then customize a solution based on your specific needs, budget, and situation.

Hourly Break-Fix Fees

Most IT services companies selling break-fix services charge between $150 and $250 per hour with a one-hour minimum. In most cases, they will give you a discount of 5% to as much as 20% on their hourly rates if you purchase and pay for a block of hours in advance. In some instances, a block of hours has a time limit before they expire — and you lose the remaining funds you paid for them.

If they are quoting a **project**, the fees range widely based on the scope of work outlined. If you are hiring an IT consulting firm for a project, I would suggest you demand the following:

- **A very detailed scope of work that specifies what "success" is.** Make sure you detail what your expectations are in performance, work flow, costs, security, access, etc.

The more detailed you can be, the better. Detailing your expectations up front will go a long way in avoiding miscommunications and additional fees later on to give you what you REALLY wanted.

- **A fixed budget and time frame for completion.** Agreeing to this up front aligns both your agenda and the consultant's. Be very wary of loose estimates that allow the consulting firm to bill you for "unforeseen" circumstances. The bottom line is this: it is your IT consulting firm's responsibility to be able to accurately assess your situation and quote a project based on their experience. You should not have to pick up the tab for a consultant underestimating a job or for their inefficiencies. A true professional knows how to take into consideration those contingencies and bill accordingly.

Managed IT Services

Most managed IT services firms will quote you a MONTHLY fee based on the number of devices they need to maintain, back up, and support. In the Fort Lee area (excluding New York City), that fee is somewhere in the range of $100 to $400 per server, $20 to $150 per desktop, and approximately $50 per smartphone or mobile device.

If you hire an IT consultant and sign up for a managed IT services contract, here are some things that SHOULD be included (make sure you read your contract to validate this):

- Security patches applied weekly, if not daily, for urgent and emerging threats
- Ancillary software patching (Adobe Reader, Flash, Java, etc.)

- Antivirus updates and monitoring
- Firewall updates and monitoring
- Backup monitoring and test restores
- Spam-filter installation and updates
- Malware detection and removal
- Monitoring disk space on workstations and servers
- Monitoring hardware for signs of failure
- Optimizing systems for maximum speed
- Quick remote support for desktops and servers
- Proper asset tracking of hardware and software
- Monthly executive reporting
- Quarterly business review
- Annual hardware review

The following services may **NOT be included** and will often be billed separately. This is not necessarily a "scam" or unethical, UNLESS the managed IT services company tries to hide these fees when selling you a service agreement. *Make sure you review your contract carefully to know what is and is NOT included!*

- Hardware, such as new servers, PCs, laptops, etc.
- Software licenses and upgrades
- On-site support
- After hours support
- Projects, like moving equipment or location
- Major changes to the existing infrastructure after the contract is signed

Warning! Gray areas of "all-inclusive" service contracts. In order to truly compare the "cost" of one managed IT services contract to another, you need to make sure you fully understand what IS and ISN'T included AND the Service Level Agreement (SLA) you are signing up for. It's VERY easy for one IT services provider to appear far less expensive than another UNTIL you look closely at what you are getting.

Chapter 9: 21 Service Clarification Questions You Should Ask Your IT Services Firm Before Signing a Contract

The following are 21 questions to ask your IT services provider that will clarify exactly what you're getting for the money. Some of these items may not be that important to you, while others (like response time, adequate insurance, and uptime guarantees) may be critical. Make sure you fully understand each of these items before making a decision about who the right provider is for you; then make sure you get this IN WRITING.

CUSTOMER SERVICE:

Q1: Do they answer their phones live, or do you always have to leave a voicemail and wait for someone to call you back?

Our Answer: I answer the phone live from 8:00 a.m. to 5:00 p.m. and give all clients an emergency after-hours number they may call if a problem arises, even on weekends. Why? Because some of the business owners I support work outside normal hours and find it the most productive time they have. If they cannot access their computer network AND can't get hold of anyone to help them, it's incredibly frustrating.

Q2: Do they offer a written, guaranteed response time to your calls?

Our Answer: I guarantee to be working on a problem within 60 minutes or less of your call. This is written into every service agreement I give to my clients because it's standard procedure.

Q3: Do they take the time to explain what they are doing and answer your questions in terms that you can understand (not geek-speak), or do they come across as arrogant and make you feel stupid for asking simple questions?

Our Answer: In college, I was an English major with a minor in education, specializing in teaching at the high school level. At the start of my computer career I was writing technical manuals. I realize that it is essential to have the "heart of a teacher," and will take time to answer your questions and explain everything in simple terms. Just look at what this one client had to say:

"I don't know how many computer consultants will tell you (or know) about all the options available to a customer. But **this one took actions that were above and beyond the basics** of computer support. I am extremely pleased with the personal service and results provided by Larry Kahm of Heliotropic Systems!"

Walter C., President
Financial Management Consulting Services firm, Fort Lee, NJ

Q4: Do they consistently (and proactively) offer new ways to improve your network's performance, or do they wait until you have a problem to make recommendations?

Our Answer: I conduct quarterly business review (QBR) meetings with my clients to look for new ways to help improve their operations, lower costs, increase efficiencies, and resolve any problems that may be arising. My goal with these meetings is to help my clients be more profitable, efficient, and competitive.

Q5: Do they provide detailed invoices that clearly explain what you are paying for?

Our Answer: I provide detailed invoices that show what work was done, why and when, so you never have to guess what you are paying for. I also double-check all invoices for accuracy before they are sent to you.

Q6: Do they have adequate Errors and Omissions insurance as well as Workers' Compensation insurance to protect YOU?

Our Answer: Here's something to consider: If THEY cause a problem with your network that causes you to be down for hours or days or to lose data, who is responsible? Here's another question to consider: If one of their technicians gets hurt at your office, who's paying? In this litigious society we live in, you better make darn sure whomever you hire is adequately insured with both Errors and Omissions insurance AND Workers' Compensation — and don't be shy about asking to see their latest insurance policies!

True Story: A few years ago Geek Squad was slapped with multimillion-dollar lawsuits from customers for bad behavior by their technicians. In some cases, their techs where accessing, copying and distributing personal information they gained access to on customers' PCs and laptops brought in for repairs. In other cases, they lost a client's laptop (and subsequently all the data on it) and tried to cover it up.

Bottom line: make sure the company you are hiring has proper insurance to protect YOU.

Q7: Do they guarantee to complete projects on time and on budget?

Our Answer: All projects are fixed-priced and guaranteed to be completed on time, in writing. This is important because many unethical or incompetent computer guys will only quote "time and materials," which gives them free rein to nickel-and-dime you, as well as take as much time as they want completing a project.

Q8: Do they insist on remotely monitoring your network 24x7x365 to keep critical security settings, virus definitions, and security patches up-to-date and PREVENT problems from turning into downtime, viruses, lost data, and other issues?

Our Answer: Yes; my remote network monitoring system watches over your network to <u>constantly</u> look for developing problems, security issues, and other problems so I can address them BEFORE they turn into bigger problems.

Q9: Do they provide you with a monthly report that shows all the updates, security patches, and status of every machine on your network so you know for SURE your systems have been secured and updated?

Our Answer: Every month my clients get a detailed report that shows an overall health score of their computers, servers, and network and the updates to their antivirus, security settings, patches and other important network checks (like hard-drive space, backups, speed and performance, etc.).

Q10: Is it standard procedure for them to provide you with written network documentation detailing what software licenses you own, critical passwords, user information, and hardware inventory or are they the only person with the "keys to the kingdom?"

Our Answer: All clients receive this in written and electronic form at no additional cost. I also perform a quarterly update on this material and make sure key people from your business have this information and know how to use it, giving you complete control over your network.

Side Note: You should NEVER allow any IT person to have that much control over you and your business. If you get the sneaking suspicion that your current IT provider is keeping this under their control as a means of job security, get rid of them (and I can help to make sure you don't suffer ANY ill effects). This is downright unethical and dangerous to your organization, so don't tolerate it!

Q11: Do they have other technicians on staff who are familiar with your network in case your regular technician goes on vacation or gets sick?

Our Answer: Yes; and because I keep detailed network documentation (basically a blueprint of your computer network) and updates on every client's account, any of my colleagues could pick up for me if I was unavailable.

Q12: When they offer an "all-inclusive" support plan, is it TRULY all-inclusive, or are their "gotchas" hidden in the fine print?

Our Answer: I do not provide an "all-inclusive" support plan, because most of my clients have not recognized the value of that kind of offering. As a result, I provide the **most amount of support** that I can for a **manageable monthly price**. However, there are certain projects — because of their very nature — that cannot be included as a fixed monthly cost. CAUTION: Make sure you REALLY understand what is and isn't included. Some things to consider are:

- Is phone/e-mail help desk included or extra?
- What about network upgrades, moves or adding/removing users?
- Is hardware and/or software included?
- What about third-party software support? (I recommend that this MUST be included.)

- What are the costs/consequences of early cancellation?
- What if you aren't happy with their services? Do they offer a money-back guarantee?
- If the hardware and software is included, what happens if you cancel the contract?
- Are off-site backups included? To what degree?
- If you have a major disaster, is restoring your network included or extra?
- What about on-site support calls? Or support to remote offices?
- Are home computers used to access the company's network after hours included or extra?
- Does the plan include all costs associated with antivirus and anti-malware?
- Does the plan include all costs associated with both local and off-site backups?
- Does the plan include test restores from the backup systems?
- Is technology management planning included?
- Are quarterly business reviews included?
- Is monitoring of the critical components included 24 hours a day and 7 days a week?
- Is periodic preventative maintenance of computers and servers included?
- Do they provide disaster recovery planning?
- Do they provide business continuity development?

BACKUPS AND DISASTER RECOVERY:

Q13: Do they INSIST on monitoring an off-site as well as an on-site back-up, or are they letting you rely on outdated tape back-ups?

Our Answer: I will *not* allow my clients to use tape back-ups, because tape back-ups are incredibly unreliable. I make sure all of my clients have a device that performs local back-ups, sends a copy of their data to the cloud, and can act as a virtual server if the real one encounters a problem. Having these abilities makes recovering files — or an entire system — smooth, fast, and stress free.

Q14: Do they INSIST on doing periodic test restores of your back-ups to make sure the data is not corrupt and could be restored in the event of a disaster?

Our Answer: My back-up software automatically checks that the image it has taken is good (and valid) before logging the end of day as complete. I perform a quarterly "fire drill" that includes a test restore from back-up for my clients to make sure their data CAN be recovered in the event of an emergency. After all, the WORST time to test a back-up is when you desperately need it.

Q15: Do they insist on backing up your network BEFORE performing any type of project or upgrade?

Our Answer: I do; and that's simply as a precaution in case a hardware failure or software glitch causes a major problem.

Q16: If you were to experience a major disaster, do they have a written plan for how your data could be restored FAST and/or enable you to work from a remote location?

Our Answer: All clients receive a simple disaster recovery plan for their data and network. I encourage them to do a full disaster recovery plan for their office, but at a minimum, their network will be covered should something happen.

TECHNICAL EXPERTISE AND SUPPORT:

Q17: Is their help-desk U.S.-based or outsourced to an overseas company or third party?

Our Answer: If you have the size requirements to warrant a help-desk to support your business, I will ensure that the one I contract out to will be US-based. I consider this one of the most important aspects of customer service, plus I feel it's important to keeping your business operating effectively.

Q18: Do their technicians maintain current vendor certifications and participate in ongoing training — or are they learning on your dime?

Our Answer: I maintain that having up-to-date education on the products and services I offer an essential part of my business. As such, I dedicate at least 10 hours each month to webinars, training sessions, and studying vendor product documentation to ensure that I can support your computers and network. In addition, I use nearly all of the software and hardware I recommend in my own office. That way I know, first hand, how they will operate in the "real world."

Q19: Do their technicians arrive on time and dress professionally?

Our Answer: I like to consider myself to be a true professional — someone that you would be proud to have in your office. I dress professionally and show up on time, and if I cannot (for some odd, unforeseen reason) make an appointment, I always notify the client immediately. I believe these are minimum requirements for delivering a professional service.

Q20: Are they familiar with (and can they support) your unique line of business applications?

Our Answer: I "own" the problems with all lines of business applications for my clients. That doesn't mean I can fix faulty software — but I WILL be the liaison between you and your vendor to resolve any problems you are having, and make sure these applications work smoothly for you.

Q21:   When something goes wrong with your Internet service, phone systems, printers or other IT services, do they take on the problem or do they say, "That's not our problem to fix"?

Our Answer: I feel I should own any IT problems for my clients so they don't have to try and resolve these issues on their own — that's just plain old good service and something many "computer guys" won't do.

Chapter 10: A Final Word and Free Assessment Offer to Show You How to Eliminate System Slowness, Crashes, and Malware and Drastically Lower Your IT Maintenance Costs

I hope you have found this book helpful in shedding some light on what to look for when hiring a professional firm to outsource your IT support to. As I stated in the opening, my purpose in providing this information was to help you make an informed decision and avoid getting burned by incompetent or unethical firms luring you in with cheap prices.

On the following pages you will find information on how to request a FREE IT Assessment for your business as a next step in engaging with us. There is no cost or obligation, and I guarantee you will find this consult to be extremely valuable and eye-opening.

I look forward to your call!

Sincerely,

Larry Kahm

Larry Kahm
President
Heliotropic Systems, Inc.
866-912-8808
www.heliotropicsystems.com

Chapter 11: Give Me 60 Minutes, and I *Guarantee* I Can Show You How to Eliminate System Slowness, Crashes, Malware, and a Host of Other Annoying IT Problems — and How to *Never Pay* For Unnecessary IT Expenses and Repairs Again

I've Got to Ask You:

- Do you have a **nagging suspicion** that your current IT provider isn't delivering the quality of service you're paying for?

- Maybe you're experiencing **chronic problems** with your computer and network systems that your IT provider just never seems to resolve.

- Maybe it has become easier to find a work-around or **try to fix IT problems yourself** than to call your IT provider.

- Or maybe you're sending a check every month for their services **but don't** *really* **know what you're paying for**. Could they really get you back up and running after a disaster? Are they *truly* maintaining critical security updates for your IT systems? Have you outgrown their ability to adequately support you?

It's very common for business owners and office managers to be unhappy with the quality of service and support they're getting from their current IT company, but they tolerate it simply because they don't know who else to call, or they're just too darn busy to take the time to find someone else.

Chapter 12: Free Customized 27-Point IT Systems Security and Performance Assessment

If I just described your situation, I want to give you a **customized IT Assessment for free** that will reveal what's REALLY going on in your computer network and show you the fastest and most efficient way to get your systems working the way they're supposed to, saving you a great deal of time, aggravation and money. **Briefly, here's what I have in mind...**

First, I want to perform our proprietary **27-Point IT Systems Security and Performance Assessment** on your computer network.

There's no charge for this, and it only requires a 60- to 90-minute meeting with me. After doing this type of thing for almost 10 years, I have perfected a process for helping businesses like *yours* to get their IT systems working the way they are supposed to.

After conducting this free IT Assessment, I'll be able to answer your top questions, such as:

- Are your IT systems truly secured from hackers, malware, and rogue employees?
- Are your backups configured properly to ensure that you could be back up and running again fast in a disaster?
- Are you unknowingly exposing your company to expensive fines and litigation under New Jersey data breach laws?
- Could you utilize cheaper and more efficient cloud-computing technologies to lower IT costs and make it easier to work remotely?

- Are your systems optimized for maximum speed and performance? (I can tell you, 99% of the computer networks I review are NOT.)

Once I have a clear picture of the state, health, and performance of your current IT systems, I'll deliver a **customized Report of Findings** that will show you how to eliminate every single nagging problem, enable you to work faster and easier, and lower IT costs wherever possible.

At the End of This Assessment, One of Three Things Will Happen

1. **You love the plan** and decide to implement it on your own. If this is the case, I'll wish you the best of luck and *ask that you keep in touch to let me know how you're doing.*

2. **You love the plan and ask to become my client so I can personally help you implement it ASAP.** *If that's the case, I will knock it out of the park… and that's a promise.*

Or finally…

3. In the unlikely and *unprecedented* event that I don't find a way to dramatically improve your situation, then you received a FREE hour of expert advice from an independent third-party who verified the security, speed, and pristine health of your computer network. To date, I have NEVER had anyone say that I've wasted their time.

Think about this…

The **worst** **that can happen** is you spend an hour having an independent third-party validate and review the security, speed, and health of your computer network.

The **best that can happen** is we work together to finally take all IT complaints off your plate.

Here's How This Will Work

First, you'll fill out a brief IT Analysis Questionnaire on our web site:

www.heliotropicsytems.com/itsurvey

This will give me the basic information I need about you and your business to prepare for our meeting.

Once you complete this, I will call you and set up a convenient time for me to come to your office and perform my **27-Point IT Systems Security and Performance Assessment**.

After that initial meeting, I will prepare a **customized Report of Findings** that will reveal any vulnerabilities in your backups and security, as well as show you how to optimize your IT to increase everyone's productivity in the fastest, most efficient way possible.

And like I said, *there's no charge for this.*

So Why Would I Offer This For Free?

For one simple reason:

It's the fastest and easiest way for me to demonstrate the value I can deliver without any risk to you. Frankly, it's how I get the happy clients you've seen all over my web site and have probably heard about before.

After all, if you like what you see and I show you how to solve a number of IT-related problems in your business, why wouldn't you want to work with me? Of course, I will approach this with no expectations or heavy sales pressure of any kind. I don't like pushy salespeople any more than you do — **and I believe that providing extreme value in advance is the best way to showcase our services** and win new business. In fact, here's my "VALUE IN ADVANCE PROMISE" to you...

You'll Find This Consultation to Be Incredibly Valuable! I Have Never Had Anyone Say That I Wasted Their Time

Now, obviously this is an amazing offer that you'll probably never see from any other IT company or computer expert in the area. But I'm SO confident that I can deliver extreme value that I have no concerns with putting this type of guarantee on our time together.

The ONLY catch is that I can't help everyone, so I have a strict (but reasonable) set of criteria that need to be met in order for me to proceed. Here it is:

1.   You have to at least have one server and five computers.

Our services and advice work best for companies that have at least one server and five computers. If that's *not* you (or if you are a brand-new startup), I might be able to help you through a different process. Call my office and I'll direct you from there: 866-912-8808.

2. You must be the owner of the business.

Due to the nature of the advice I will be giving you, it will be actionable only for the owner or key executive.

If You Meet the Criteria Above, Here's How We Get Started:

Step 1: Go to the web site below to complete an IT Analysis Questionnaire. Don't worry, it's simple and unobtrusive:

www.heliotropicsytems.com/itsurvey

Step 2: After I receive your application and review it, I will personally call you and set up a time for us to meet.

The initial meeting will take between 60 and 90 minutes. This is where we really begin working to figure out exactly what you want and how to make it happen. We'll also initiate our **27-Point IT Systems Security and Performance Assessment.**

Step 3: After that initial meeting, I'll prepare a **customized Report of Findings** that will reveal any vulnerability in your backups and security, as well as show you how to optimize your IT to increase everyone's productivity in the fastest, most efficient way possible. <u>This second meeting should be a real eye-opener for you.</u>

If you see the value in engaging beyond that, great! We can talk about it at that time. And if you don't want to become a client — *that's OK too*. By the way, I've *never* had anyone feel like their time was wasted. EVER. That's why I can make this offer. WE DELIVER.

So, unless you are 100% happy with the IT support you are getting and absolutely confident that your network is secure, backed up properly and running at optimal levels, why wouldn't you give this a try? **Do it now and you'll be glad you did:**

www.heliotropicsystems.com/itsurvey

Chapter 13: The Top Seven Reasons Why You'll Want to Outsource Your IT Support to Us

Here is what I promise to deliver when you select Heliotropic Systems to service your business' computers and network:

1. Rapid Response – When you call about a computer or network problem, I guarantee that your phone call will be answered immediately, or returned within 60 minutes or less. I know you're busy, and have made a sincere commitment to making sure your computer problems get fixed quickly. And because most issues can be handled remotely (using our secure management tools), you don't have to wait around for a technician to show up.

2. No Geek Speak – You deserve to get answers to your questions *in plain English*, not in confusing technical terms. I will not talk down to you or make you feel stupid because you don't understand how all this "technology" works. That's my job!

3. Projects Are Completed On Time And On Budget – When you hire me to complete a project for you, I won't nickel-and-dime you with unforeseen or unexpected charges or delays. I will deliver precisely what I promised to deliver, on time and on budget, with no excuses.

4. Peace Of Mind – Because I monitor all of my clients' networks 24x7x365, you never have to worry that malware has spread, a hacker has broken in, or a backup has failed. I watch over your entire network, taking the management and hassle of maintaining it off your hands. This frees you to focus on *your*

39

customers and running *your* business; not on your IT systems.

5. Business Savvy – I design, evaluate, and implement technology solutions based on a thorough understanding of the benefits they will provide to *your* business.

6. I Won't Hold You Hostage – Many IT companies do NOT provide their clients with simple and easy-to-understand documentation that outlines key network resources, passwords, licenses, etc. By keeping that to themselves, IT companies hold their clients "hostage" to scare them away from hiring someone else. This is both unethical and unprofessional. As a client, I will provide you with full written documentation of your network and all the resources, software licenses, passwords, and hardware in simple terms so you can understand it. I keep my clients by delivering outstanding IT support and services — not by keeping them in the dark.

7. 100% No-Small-Print Satisfaction Guarantee – You deserve a fully functioning computer system. If, at any point, a problem arises and you are not happy with my efforts to correct it, please let me know so that I can do everything possible to remedy the situation. If I cannot re-solve the problem to your satisfaction, you are entitled to a 100% refund – <u>no</u> questions, <u>no</u> hassles.

Appendix A: Quiz – How to Choose Your IT Model

You may be the type of business owner who knows right away which kind of IT support is right for you. But for some, it's a challenge to weigh the cost against the support you're going to receive.

To assist you, here is an 8-question quiz that will let you determine which model is best for you. Give yourself a 1 if the question isn't important for your business, a 5 if you feel it's essential, or a 2, 3 or 4 if you're somewhere in the middle.

With the help of my IT team, do I want to…

1. _____ find out immediately if my data back-up fails to run?

2. _____ know which equipment on my network is aging and might need replacing in the next 6 - 12 months?

3. _____ know if my server and all of my desktops have the latest anti-virus updates installed and are functioning correctly?

4. _____ know if the latest security patches have been installed on my network?

5. _____ know who the heaviest Internet users are, and whether they are downloading large files that can slow down the network, or accessing inappropriate web sites?

6. _____ know which computers are running out of memory, affecting user performance?

7. _____ know if my firewall settings are correctly configured to protect my network?

8. _____ have one number to call for all of my technology service requirements?

If you gave each question a 3 or higher, then you're seeing how important a dedicated managed services IT provider is to your business, and why it's worth the investment. The fact of the matter is computer networks absolutely, positively, need ongoing maintenance and monitoring to stay secure.

Keeping your systems up and running, which is what managed IT services is all about, is a LOT less expensive and damaging to your organization than waiting until something bad happens, and then paying for emergency IT services to restore your systems to working order.

About the Author and Heliotropic Systems

Larry Kahm created Heliotropic Systems more than 20 years ago to work as a consultant at Fortune 100 companies. During that time he provided support to application programmers, systems programmers, and management. As part of his responsibilities he wrote custom code, developed and documented dozens of procedures, and conducted presentations for hundreds of staff.

The overarching set of skills he developed consisted of listening to requirements, understanding the business' needs, and then devising solutions that matched those criteria.

Following the economic meltdown of 2008 he bid farewell to the major corporate environment. He saw that small businesses and entrepreneurs were being ignored or underserved by existing computer support companies. So he decided to specialize in providing quick response, reliable solutions, and extraordinary customer service to a marketplace that had rarely experienced that kind of service. Larry recognized they were working furiously to keep their business running, and they didn't want to be bothered with problems that invariably came up with using computers.

When asked what's most important to his new-found role, he frequently responds, "I want business owners to get the most out of their technology, and to ensure that their computer systems just plain work." Over the years, Heliotropic Systems has help dozens of clients relieve their technology worries so that they can concentrate on growing and realizing their business goals.

Heliotropic Systems' growth is based on Larry's attention to delivering outstanding computer support to his clients.

Now when he meets with business owners, he continues to listen carefully as they describe their business goals. "What is extremely important to me is that I am helping others solve puzzles with the skills and knowledge that I have acquired over the years. My clients benefit by having an available resource to answer their questions, and they know that their computer systems are protected."

www.ingramcontent.com/pod-product-compliance
Lightning Source LLC
Chambersburg PA
CBHW021927170526
45157CB00005B/2214